School Days Long Ago

A Division of The McGraw·Hill Companies

Columbus, Ohio

www.sra4kids.com

SRA/McGraw-Hill

A Division of The **McGraw·Hill** *Companies*

Send all inquiries to:
SRA/McGraw-Hill
8787 Orion Place
Columbus, OH 43240-4027

ISBN 0-07-571792-1
  2 3 4 5 6 7 8 9 DBH 05 04 03 02

One-Room Schoolhouse

Can you imagine going to school in 1776? That was a long, long time ago—more than 200 years ago, in fact. Getting an education was very different back then.

Schools in those days were very small. Most had only a single room. One teacher taught all the children. Students were in grades one through eight and were from six to twenty years old. Enrollment was usually small.

The teacher arrived early to sweep and clean the entire classroom. In winter, the building was kept warm with a fireplace or a wood-burning stove. Parents provided the firewood. Each morning, a different student would start the fire before the other children arrived.

Before coming to school, many children had chores to do at home. The environment was harsh. The children walked miles to school or rode horses. There were no school buses, cars, or pavement.

A Dog will bite
A Thief at night.

One book, called a primer, contained the alphabet, numbers, spelling words, and poems. During the first part of the day, the teacher worked with the younger ones. Older students worked on their own, studying and writing in their copybooks by themselves. Copybook paper had no lines. Students had to draw their own straight lines on the paper before they could write.

Good penmanship, or neat handwriting, was an important skill for a farmer, storekeeper, or craftsperson. Children used a slate pencil to copy their writing lesson from the blackboard onto a small slate. Later, they used a quill pen and an inkpot to copy it into their copybooks in their best handwriting.

Later in the afternoon, older students
worked on spelling, reading, and arithmetic
while younger ones practiced the alphabet.
Because paper and books were scarce, students
learned to do addition, subtraction, division,
and multiplication in their heads.

Children carried their lunches in tin pails or baskets, or tied in cloth. Homemade bread and jam were packed. Drinking water came from the well.

At recess, games were often made up and needed little equipment. Leftover wood and string were used to make spinning tops. Hoops from barrels were used in races and other games.

Girls liked to play hopscotch, sing songs, and play with cornhusk dolls. The boys played marbles, tag, or football. Football was a rough game and was played with a stuffed leather sack. The children also liked to play hide-and-seek.

After school, children went home and did their evening chores. Then the family ate supper and spent the evening together. Bedtime was welcome after such a long day. The children would need a good night's rest to rise at dawn to begin a new day.

16